CONTENTS

INTRODUCTION

Automate Your Financial Life in 7 Days: A Behavioral Guide for Good Stewards

Financial management can often seem daunting, but with the right steps, you can automate your financial life in just seven days. This guide will provide practical steps to streamline your finances and use biblical principles to emphasize the importance of being a good steward.

In a country that prioritizes capitalism and one that gained the foundation of its wealth from the slave labor of other human beings, the topic of personal finance and wealth is deeply personal to me. We don't all start from the same point, however, the other side to this peculiar experiment we call America is that being born into poverty is not a state that we are permanently relegated to.
Somewhere along my journey, I heard the phrase *"It's more expensive to be poor"*. Understanding that concept eluded me for a long time.
By this point, you may be wondering who I am. My name is Richard Frierson and I'm a financial coach. Maybe, more importantly, I'm an ordinary W-2 wage-earning American from an underserved section of the country. I hit a significant financial milestone by the age of 45 but missed the mark of the intended

goal: retirement. I share that point for a couple reasons.

1. It wasn't a number that I was targeting, but to be able to retire. My mindset up until I was 34 was full of distractions and impoverished thinking
2. That number and milestone only have significance to me.

I learned this when I shared this goal with a few people. I got different responses, 1 guy immediately directed my attention to an even richer classmate, and another ghosted me for almost a year until I decided to reach out after months of missed calls.

I share all of this to let you know that as a person on their journey as well as being a financial coach, I have much lived experience in the areas of finance, business, relational trauma, and mindset shifting, that's gifted me the passion to empower others. When you are on your journey, utilize discernment with who you share your successes, even defeats. Your goals will be personal, realize not everyone is on the same journey. Seek out the folks who are excited for you and don't get discouraged by the ones who are not.

With that out of the way, let's get back to it. My family has reduced stress when it comes to finances, we don't fight over money when groceries are high or when a car repair is needed. Our lifestyle is not lavish but our mindset has grown immensely. I'd like to share some of these lessons with you. For some, it may be sooner than I learned and later for others, but the good thing about sound principles; they work whenever you put them to use.

Let's get back to understanding how to Learn, Build and Grow!

They are hidden; elusive may be a better word; poverty costs: Let's take a moment to explore why it's more expensive to be poor.

At first glance, this might seem contradictory. How can having less money cost more? Yet, when we delve deeper into the everyday realities faced by those with limited financial resources, it becomes clear that poverty comes with hidden costs that make it difficult to get ahead. These elusive costs contribute to the cycles that keep people trapped in poverty, but there are actionable steps to help break free.

Poverty becomes a cycle that we only escape from with intention:

When you're struggling to make ends meet, every decision carries more weight, and the margin for error is razor-thin. This creates a cycle where short-term solutions lead to long-term costs.

Let's explore some of these costs and how they rear their head.

1. High Interest Rates, Modern Debt Traps and their Fees:

Buy Now, Pay Later (BNPL) Services (Afterpay, Affirm, Klarna, etc.):

- These installment payment plans may seem like a convenient way to spread out purchases, but they can create a false sense of affordability. Many users accumulate multiple BNPL obligations at once, leading to payment overload. Missed or late payments often come with high fees, and some services report to credit bureaus, potentially impacting your credit score.

Credit Cards and Pay-Over-Time Features:

- Credit card companies now offer "pay over time" options on purchases, often at interest rates well above 20%. While this may feel like a structured repayment plan, it can lead to excessive interest costs if balances are not paid in full. Introductory 0% APR offers can also be dangerous if the balance isn't cleared before the promotional period ends, as high retroactive interest may apply.

Payday Loans and High-Interest Short-Term Lending:

- Payday loans remain one of the most predatory lending options, with APRs reaching 400% or more. These loans trap borrowers in cycles of debt, where they continually roll over payments and pay excessive fees, making it nearly impossible to break free.

Auto-Title and Predatory Personal Loans:

- Loans that require your car title or charge ultra-high interest rates on small amounts can quickly spiral out of control. Defaulting on a title loan can lead to losing your vehicle, adding to financial distress.

Overdraft Fees:

- Those living paycheck to paycheck are more likely to overdraw their accounts, leading to costly overdraft fees. A $35 fee might not seem like much, but if it happens multiple times, it can quickly add up to hundreds of dollars a year.

2. Higher Costs for Essentials:

Buying in Small Quantities:

- Those with limited cash flow often have to buy groceries and other essentials in small quantities, which tend to be more expensive per unit. For example, buying a small pack of paper towels or a single roll is more expensive than buying in bulk.

No Access to Discounts:

- When you can't afford to buy in bulk or take advantage of sales (because you don't have extra money), you miss out on savings that are available to those with more financial flexibility.

3. Poor Housing Options:

- Nuanced View of Housing Options:
    - **Renting vs. Owning:**
        - Renting and owning both have advantages depending on individual circumstances, market conditions, and financial goals. While homeownership often allows you to build equity and can be a long-term wealth-building tool, it's not always the best option for everyone. In some markets, renting can be more affordable and provide flexibility, especially for those who aren't

ready to commit to a specific location or have uncertain job prospects.

- On the other hand, renting doesn't provide the opportunity to build equity directly, and rising rents can make long-term affordability challenging. However, renting can free up cash flow for other investments, particularly in high-cost markets where homeownership may not be feasible or financially prudent.

Energy Inefficiency:

- Rental properties, particularly older ones, may lack energy-efficient features, leading to higher utility bills. While renters may not have the ability to make significant upgrades, they can often negotiate with landlords for improvements or choose rentals with better energy standards.
- For owners, energy efficiency upgrades require upfront investment but can yield long-term savings. Renters benefit from avoiding these costs while remaining flexible to move if their housing costs or circumstances change.
- Renting is not inherently a poor financial choice—it's a matter of aligning housing decisions with your current financial situation, goals, and lifestyle. Both renting and owning come with trade-offs, and the best option depends on individual priorities and the housing market at the time.

4. Limited Access to Affordable Health Care:

- **Preventative Care:** Without insurance or the means to pay out-of-pocket, regular check-ups and preventative care are often skipped, leading to more severe health problems and higher medical bills down the road.

\- Emergency Expenses: Health issues that could have been managed with early intervention often turn into emergencies, requiring expensive treatments that can push a family into deeper financial hardship.

5. Transportation Costs:

- Unreliable Transportation: When you can't afford a reliable car or live in an area without good public transportation, getting to work or school can be a challenge. This can lead to missed opportunities, job instability, and additional costs for repairs or alternative transportation.
- High Insurance Rates: Those with poor credit or living in high-risk areas often pay more for car insurance, even if they're good drivers.

This book is intended to be an intentional guide for a beginner who is looking to break free from the cycle of poverty and the challenges that come along with it. I reassure you, that it is possible with a strategic approach.

Here are a few steps to consider as we explore expanding your mindset:

1. Build an Emergency Fund:

- Start Small: Begin by saving a small amount each month, even if it's just $10 or $20. Over time, this will build up and provide a cushion against unexpected expenses.
- Automate Savings: Set up automatic transfers to a savings account to ensure consistency. Even small contributions add up over time.

2. Access Affordable Financial Products:

- Credit Unions: Look for local credit unions, which often offer lower interest rates and fees than traditional banks or payday lenders.

- Community Programs: Investigate community-based programs that offer financial literacy classes, low-interest loans, or assistance with banking services.

3. Maximize Your Income:
   - Skill Development: Consider investing in your education or skills training. Community colleges, online courses, and local nonprofits often offer affordable or free options.
   - Side Hustles: Explore side gigs or part-time work to supplement your income. Platforms like Fiverr, Uber, or TaskRabbit offer flexible opportunities to earn extra cash.

4. Prioritize Health and Wellness:
   - Utilize Community Health Resources: Many communities offer free or low-cost clinics. Take advantage of these for preventative care and routine check-ups.
   - Healthy Living on a Budget: Invest in your health by choosing affordable, nutritious food options and engaging in regular exercise, which can prevent costly medical bills in the long run.

5. Reduce High-Cost Debt:
   - Debt Repayment Strategies: Focus on paying down high-interest debt first, like payday loans or credit cards. Consider the snowball or avalanche methods to tackle debt systematically.
   - Consolidate Debt: Look into debt consolidation options, which might lower your interest rate and simplify payments.

6. Seek Better Housing Options:
   - Housing Assistance Programs: Investigate local housing assistance programs, including those that help with rent, and utility bills, or offer paths to homeownership.

- Energy Efficiency Grants: Some states and local governments offer grants or low-interest loans to help with home energy improvements.

7. Leverage Social Support :
    - Community and Government Resources: A Step Toward Stability
        - It's important to recognize that seeking assistance when needed is not a sign of failure—it's a strategic step toward improving your situation. Many communities offer valuable resources designed to provide temporary support while you work toward long-term stability. These may include food banks, job training programs, childcare assistance, and other services.
        - The key is to approach these resources with the right mindset. View them as tools to help you bridge the gap, not as a permanent solution. Honestly assess your situation, create a plan, and take calculated steps toward financial independence. Seeking help when necessary allows you to focus on building a stronger foundation, improving your skills, and positioning yourself for future success.

Remember, utilizing available resources with a mindset of growth and responsibility can be a powerful way to improve your circumstances and achieve your goals.

8. Educate Yourself on Personal Finance:
    - Books and Online Resources: Take advantage of free or low-cost personal finance books, podcasts, and websites that offer practical advice on budgeting, saving, and investing.

- Financial Coaching: If possible, consider working with a financial coach who can help you create a personalized plan to achieve financial stability.

The saying ***"it's more expensive to be poor"*** reflects the harsh reality that those with fewer financial resources often face higher costs and more obstacles to achieving financial security. However, by understanding these hidden costs and taking proactive steps, it's possible to break free from the cycle of poverty and move toward a more stable and prosperous future. Remember, the journey out of poverty is not just about making more money—it's about making smart, informed decisions that build a solid financial foundation over time. Let's dive into some age-old wisdom in the following chapters that can guide your actions on this journey to a more intentional and impactful life.

One more thing before we dive in. Just like money, **this book is a tool**. Like any tool, it's much more useful to us when we're taught how to use it. At the beginning of each chapter, you'll find a biblical passage to highlight the principle. There will be a step-by-step so you have an easy reference back to what actionable steps you can take to reinforce the principle. Additionally, you'll find prompts and reflections throughout. It's best to take your time and pull out a notepad and pen now so that you can take action immediately. If you do these things, you will gain the maximum use of this tool.

CHAPTER 1: SETTING FINANCIAL GOALS

"For which of you, intending to build a tower, does not sit down first and count the cost, whether he has enough to finish it" (Luke 14:28).

Step-by-Step:

1. *Define Short-Term and Long-Term Goals: Identify what you want to achieve in the next year, five years, and ten years.*
2. *Write Them Down: Document your goals to make them tangible and keep them visible as a daily reminder.*
3. *Prioritize: Decide which goals are most important and need immediate attention.*

Why Financial Goals Matter

Have you ever found yourself wondering where all your money goes each month? Or maybe you've thought about the future and felt a little anxious because you're not sure how you'll reach the life you want. These feelings are more common than you might think. Many people live paycheck to paycheck, not because they don't have enough money, but because they haven't taken the time to set clear financial goals.

Setting financial goals is like creating a blueprint for your future. It's not just about having more money—it's about having a plan for your money that aligns with the life you want to build. When you write down your goals, you give them power. You turn vague dreams into concrete steps that can guide your decisions and keep you focused.

And here's the good news: It's okay if your goals change over time. As you grow and your life evolves, your financial goals should too. This is an ongoing process, one that will help you stay on track, even as your circumstances and priorities shift.

The Story of Mark and His New Beginning

Let's take a moment to think about a story from scripture. In Luke 14:28, Jesus says, "For which of you, desiring to build a tower, does not first sit down and count the cost, whether he has enough to complete it?" This verse is often used to emphasize the importance of planning. It's a reminder that before starting any project—whether it's building a tower or planning your financial future—you need to have a clear understanding of what it will take to achieve your goal.

Mark had never really thought much about financial goals. He lived day to day, paying his bills as they came and occasionally saving a little when he could. He wasn't rich, but he wasn't struggling either. He just didn't think financial goals were for him—after all, he didn't have a lot of money to work with, so what was the point?

One day, Mark's car broke down. It wasn't the first time, but this time it was serious. The repairs were going to cost more than the car was worth. Mark didn't have enough savings to buy a new car, and he didn't want to take on more debt. He felt stuck, frustrated, and a bit ashamed that he hadn't been more prepared.

That night, Mark thought about what had happened and remembered the verse from Luke 14:28. He realized that he had been trying to build his life without ever counting the cost or making a plan. He decided it was time to change that.

Mark started by writing down his financial goals. At first, they were simple—save for a new car, pay off credit card debt, and build an emergency fund. But as he wrote them down, he began to see beyond just the immediate needs. He started to think about his long-term goals, like buying a house and eventually retiring. For the first time, he felt like he was in control of his future.

As the months went by, Mark found that having written goals made a big difference. Whenever he was tempted to spend money impulsively, he thought about his goals and made choices that aligned with them instead. He also realized that as his life changed, so did his goals. After paying off his debt and saving for the car, he began to focus on investing for retirement. His goals evolved, but his commitment to planning and staying focused remained strong.

The Importance of Writing Down Your Goals

Writing down your financial goals is powerful for several reasons:

- **Clarity:** Putting your goals on paper forces you to be clear about what you want to achieve. It takes your ideas out of your head and makes them real and tangible.

- **Focus:** Written goals help you stay focused. When you know what you're working toward, it's easier to make decisions that support your goals, rather than getting sidetracked by distractions.
- **Motivation:** Seeing your goals in writing can be incredibly motivating. It's a reminder of why you're making sacrifices today for a better tomorrow.
- **Accountability:** Written goals provide a level of accountability. They're a commitment you make to yourself, and having them in writing makes it harder to ignore them.
- **Adaptability:** As you grow and change, your goals should too. Writing them down allows you to periodically review and adjust them to reflect your current priorities and circumstances.

Setting Your Financial Goals: A Template And Exercise

Now that you understand the importance of setting financial goals, it's time to start creating your own. Let's take a look at a template and some prompts to help you get started today.

Financial Goals Template:

Short-Term Goals (1 year or less):

- Example: Save $1,000 for an emergency fund.
- Example: Pay off $500 in credit card debt.
- Example: Save $500 for a vacation.

Medium-Term Goals (1-5 years):

- Example: Save $10,000 for a down payment on a house.
- Example: Pay off all remaining credit card debt.
- Example: Save for a new car.

Long-Term Goals (5+ years):

- Example: Save $100,000 for retirement.
- Example: Pay off student loans.
- Example: Build a college fund for your children.

Exercise: Writing Down Your Goals

Start with Reflection:

- Think about where you are in your life right now. What are your biggest financial challenges? What are your hopes for the future? How would you like your financial situation to improve?

Prioritize Your Goals:

- Start by listing all the financial goals you can think of, big and small. Once you have your list, rank them in order of importance. What goals will have the biggest impact on your life? Which ones can wait?

Set Specific, Measurable Goals:

- Make your goals as specific as possible. For example, instead of saying "save money," say "save $5,000 by the end of the year." This gives you a clear target to work toward.

Break Down Large Goals:

- Large goals can be overwhelming, so break them down into smaller, more manageable steps. For example, if your goal is to save $10,000 for a down payment on a house, start by setting a monthly savings goal.

Write Them Down:

- Use the template above to write down your short-term, medium-term, and long-term financial goals. Be specific and include target dates for each goal.

Review and Adjust:

- Every few months, review your goals. Are you making progress? Do any of your goals need to be adjusted? Remember, it's okay to change your goals as your life and priorities evolve.

Conclusion: Building Your Financial Future

Setting financial goals is one of the most important steps you can take to build a secure and fulfilling future. It's not just about having more money—it's about making sure your money is working for you, helping you achieve the things that matter most. Remember, your goals are a reflection of your values and priorities. As you grow and change, so will your goals, and that's perfectly okay. The important thing is to keep moving forward, one step at a time, with a clear vision of the life you want to create. So take a moment, sit down, and start writing your goals. This is your blueprint, your roadmap to a better future. And with each goal you set and achieve, you're building the life you've always dreamed of.

CHAPTER 2: CREATING A VISION FOR YOUR FINANCIAL LIFE

"The plans of the diligent lead surely to plenty, but those of everyone who is hasty, surely to poverty" (Proverbs 21:5). Planning and diligence are key to financial success.

Step-by-Step:

1. *Track Your Spending: Review your bank statements and receipts to understand your current spending habits.*
2. *Categorize Expenses: Group your expenses into categories such as housing, food, transportation, and entertainment.*
3. *Set Limits: Based on your income, set spending limits for each category.*

A Common Struggle

Let's be honest—when most people hear the word "budget," they cringe. It conjures up images of restriction, of saying "no" to the things we want, and of living a life where we're constantly counting pennies. It feels like a chore, a burden, or even a punishment. But what if I told you that budgeting isn't about restriction? What if I told you that it's not even about money? Instead, it's about making choices that reflect what truly matters to you.

Let me share a story with you—one that might sound familiar.

The Story of Lisa and Her "Plan"

Lisa was like many of us. She had a decent job, paid her bills on time, and enjoyed life's little luxuries—a daily latte, weekend dinners out, and the occasional impulse buy. But every month, as she watched her bank account balance dip lower and lower, she felt a familiar pang of anxiety. Where was all her money going? Why did she always feel like she was running out of cash before the next paycheck?

Whenever someone suggested she start budgeting, Lisa's reaction was immediate: "No thanks, I don't want to feel like I'm depriving myself." To her, budgeting meant cutting back on everything that made life enjoyable. It felt like a straightjacket, confining her to a life of saying "no" to all the things she loved.

But one day, Lisa had a conversation with her friend Rachel, who had just started using a different approach to managing her money. Rachel didn't call it budgeting. Instead, she called it her "Life Plan."

Intrigued, Lisa asked what made this so different from a budget. Rachel explained, "A Life Plan isn't about restriction. It's about making intentional choices that align with what's important to you. It's not about how much you earn or spend—it's about how you choose to use your money to live the life you want."

This idea resonated with Lisa. It shifted her focus from the negative—what she would have to give up—to the positive: what she could gain by making better choices. So, Lisa decided to give it a try.

Shifting the Focus: From Budgeting to Life Planning

The first thing Lisa did was sit down and think about what truly mattered to her. She realized that while she loved her daily latte and dinners out, there were other things she valued more—like traveling, saving for a future home, and eventually starting her own business. These were the things that would bring her long-term happiness, far more than the fleeting pleasure of a fancy coffee or a new pair of shoes.

So, Lisa started her Life Plan. She didn't focus on cutting back; she focused on redirecting her money toward what mattered most. She began by setting aside a small amount each month for her travel fund. She also decided to reduce her spending on things that weren't as important. Instead of going out to dinner every weekend, she chose to cook at home more often, and surprisingly, she found that she enjoyed it. She still treated herself to a latte, but only on Fridays, making it a special end-of-week ritual rather than a daily habit.

As Lisa continued with her Life Plan, something incredible happened. She started to feel more in control of her money, rather than feeling like her money controlled her. She watched her savings grow, and with it, her confidence. For the first time, she felt like she was moving towards her goals, not just treading water.

And here's the kicker—Lisa never felt deprived. Instead, she felt empowered because every dollar she spent was a choice, not an obligation.

The Moral of the Story: It's About Choices, Not Money

Lisa's story illustrates a simple truth: it's not the amount of money you have that determines your financial well-being—it's the choices you make with it. Money is just a tool, a reflection of our priorities and decisions. When we approach our finances with intention, focusing on what truly matters, we can create a life that brings us fulfillment and joy, rather than one that's dictated by stress and scarcity.

So, let's replace the word "budget" with all its negative connotations and embrace a new term: Life Plan. Your Life Plan isn't about saying "no" to everything; it's about saying "yes" to the things that matter most. It's about taking control of your money, not the other way around.

How to Start Your Life Plan

Identify Your Priorities:

- What are the things that truly matter to you? Is it financial security, experiences like travel, building a family, or starting a business? Write them down.

Evaluate Your Spending:

- Take a look at where your money is going now. Are you spending on things that don't align with your priorities? Where can you redirect your money to better reflect what you value?

Set Specific Goals:

- Based on your priorities, set specific goals. How much do you need to save each month to fund a vacation or start an emergency fund? Break it down into manageable steps.

Automate and Simplify:

- Automate savings and bill payments where possible. This reduces the mental burden of managing money and ensures that your Life Plan stays on track.

Review and Adjust:

- Your Life Plan isn't set in stone. Review it regularly and make adjustments as your priorities and life circumstances change.

Conclusion: Your Life, Your Plan

At the end of the day, your financial well-being is about more than just numbers on a spreadsheet. It's about living a life that reflects your values, your goals, and your dreams. When you approach your finances with this mindset, you're not just managing money—you're crafting a life that's rich in meaning and purpose.

So, embrace your Life Plan, make intentional choices, and watch as your money starts to work for you, not against you. Remember, it's not about how much you have—it's about what you do with it that counts.

CHAPTER 3: AUTOMATING SAVINGS:

The Key To A Life Of Abundance

"Precious treasure and oil are in a wise man's dwelling, but a foolish man devours it" (Proverbs 21:20). Saving is wise and ensures preparedness for the future.

Step-by-Step:

1. *Open a Savings Account: If you don't have one, open a dedicated savings account.*
2. *Set Up Automatic Transfers: Arrange for a portion of your income to be automatically transferred to your savings account each payday.*
3. *Emergency Fund: Aim to save at least three to six months' worth of expenses for emergencies.*

The Wisdom Of Saving

When it comes to personal finance, one of the simplest yet most powerful strategies is automating your savings. It might seem like a small action, but the impact it can have on your financial well-being—and your overall quality of life—cannot be overstated. Automating your savings ensures that you're consistently setting aside money for the future without even having to think about it. The beauty of this process is that it not only helps you build wealth over time but also frees up mental energy, reduces stress, and allows you to focus on other important aspects of your life.

Let's begin by looking at a piece of timeless wisdom from the Bible: Proverbs 21:20 says, "The wise store up choice food and olive oil, but fools gulp theirs down." This verse captures the essence of saving. The wise make a habit of storing resources for the future, while those who fail to plan live day-to-day, consume all they have. In a modern context, this scripture speaks to the importance of creating a financial cushion—building savings that will support you during life's inevitable ups and downs.

Automating your savings is the ultimate tool for ensuring that you're living like the wise. It's an effortless way to "store up" resources for the future, and the benefits extend far beyond just your bank account.

The Power of Automating Your Savings

When you automate your savings, you are making a deliberate choice to prioritize your future. It's like putting your financial plan on autopilot, allowing you to make consistent progress toward your goals without having to make repeated decisions. Here's why automating your savings is so powerful:

Consistency Without Effort:

- When you automate, you remove the need for willpower or constant decision-making. You don't have to rely on discipline to transfer money into your savings account each month—it happens automatically, like clockwork. This consistency is key to building long-term financial security.

Pay Yourself First:

- Automating your savings ensures that you pay yourself first, before any other expenses. Too often, people try to save whatever is left over at the end of the month, only to find there's nothing left. By setting up automatic transfers, you guarantee that your savings goals are met before you have a chance to spend.

The Magic of Compound Interest:

- By saving regularly, you allow your money to grow over time through the power of compound interest. Even small amounts, when saved consistently, can grow significantly. This exponential growth is the key to building wealth and achieving long-term financial goals, whether it's buying a house, retiring comfortably, or funding your children's education.

Reduces Stress and Mental Load:

- When your savings are automated, you no longer have to worry about whether you're putting enough aside each month. This reduces financial stress and frees up mental energy. With one less thing to think about, you can focus on more important areas of your life, like your relationships, health, and personal growth.

Prepares You for the Unexpected:

- Life is unpredictable, and unexpected expenses are bound to happen. Automating your savings helps you build an emergency fund that will protect you in times of financial stress. Whether it's a medical emergency, car repair, or job loss, having a safety net can prevent you from falling into debt or financial ruin.

The Ripple Effect: How Automated Savings Optimize Your Life Beyond Finances

Automating your savings does more than just secure your financial future—it has a ripple effect that can improve other areas of your life. Here's how automating your savings can optimize your life beyond just dollars and cents:

Less Worry, More Peace of Mind:

- When your savings are automated, you no longer have to worry about whether you're saving enough for the future. This peace of mind allows you to be more present in your daily life, free from the stress of constantly managing your finances. Knowing that you're consistently working toward your financial goals can help you sleep better at night and feel more secure overall.

Increased Focus on Personal Growth:

- With the mental burden of saving off your shoulders, you can focus more on self-improvement and personal growth. Whether it's pursuing a new skill, investing in your education, or simply having more time for your family and hobbies, automated savings frees you up to invest in yourself and your well-being.

Building Confidence and Discipline:

- Automating your savings may seem like a simple act, but it builds financial discipline over time. By consistently setting aside money for the future, you're developing habits of financial responsibility and control. This discipline can spill over into other areas of life, from managing your time more effectively to making healthier choices.

The Freedom to Pursue Dreams:

- With savings consistently growing in the background, you're building a foundation that gives you the freedom to pursue bigger dreams. Whether it's starting your own business, traveling the world, or retiring early, automated savings help make these dreams possible by ensuring that you're financially prepared.

Living a Values-Driven Life:

- Proverbs 21:20 teaches us that wise people store up resources not just for themselves, but for the benefit of others. When you automate your savings, you're able to plan for generosity. This might mean giving to a cause you care about, helping a family member in need, or supporting your community. Financial security allows you to live according to your values, focusing less on survival and more on contributing to the world around you.

How to Automate Your Savings: A Simple Guide

If you're ready to experience the exponential benefits of automated savings, here's a simple guide to help you get started:

Open a Dedicated Savings Account:

- Start by opening a separate savings account, preferably one that earns interest. Having a separate account will make it easier to track your progress and keep your savings out of sight and out of mind.

Set a Savings Goal:

- Whether it's an emergency fund, a vacation, or a down payment on a home, decide what you're saving for. Knowing your goal will help keep you motivated.

Calculate a Monthly Savings Amount:

- Take a look at your monthly income and expenses. Decide how much you can comfortably set aside each month. Even if it's just a small amount, remember that consistency is what matters.

Set Up an Automatic Transfer:

- Go to your bank's website or app and set up an automatic transfer from your checking account to your savings account. Schedule the transfer for a day right after you get paid to ensure that your savings are prioritized before other expenses.

Adjust and Increase Over Time:

- As your financial situation improves or your income increases, adjust your automatic savings amount. Aim to increase it over time to accelerate your progress toward your goals.

Conclusion: Wisdom for Your Future

Proverbs 21:20 reminds us of the wisdom in storing up resources for the future. By automating your savings, you are taking a step toward living that wisdom every day. The act of saving might seem small, but its impact on your life is exponential. It brings peace of mind, financial security, and the freedom to focus on what truly matters.

In the end, automating your savings is about more than just money—it's about building a life of abundance, not just in financial terms but in every area of your life. So take the first step, set up your automated savings, and start experiencing the ripple effect of this powerful, life-changing habit.

CHAPTER 4: BILL PAYMENTS ON AUTO

"Owe no one anything, except to love each other, for the one who loves another has fulfilled the law" (Romans 13:8). Keeping up with your bills ensures you owe nothing and maintain good relationships.

Step-by-Step:
Steps to Automate Your Bill Payments

1. ***List Your Bills:***
    a. *Create a list of all your recurring bills, including due dates and amounts. Include utilities, rent/ mortgage, loans, credit cards, subscriptions, and insurance premiums.*
2. ***Set Up Automation:***
    a. *Use your bank's online bill pay service or set up autopay directly with your service providers. Schedule payments for a date that aligns with your paycheck to ensure funds are available.*
3. ***Track and Monitor:***
    a. *Even with automation, review your accounts regularly to ensure payments are processed correctly and there are no errors.*
4. ***Keep a Buffer:***
    a. *Maintain a cushion in your checking account to cover unexpected fluctuations in expenses or*

timing issues.

5. ***Adjust as Needed:***
    a. *If your financial situation changes, update your automated payments to reflect new due dates or amounts.*

Pay On Time, Live In Peace: The Power Of Automating Bills And Debt Freedom

The Weight Of Debt

Have you ever felt the anxiety of watching the due date for a bill creep closer, knowing you haven't set aside the money to pay it? Or the guilt of receiving a late notice and realizing you've let something slip through the cracks? For many, managing bills and debt can feel like a never-ending cycle of stress.

The Bible offers us wisdom in this area. Romans 13:8 says, *"Owe no one anything, except to love each other, for the one who loves another has fulfilled the law."* This verse reminds us that keeping up with our financial obligations isn't just about money—it's about relationships and living in harmony. When we pay our bills on time and work toward getting out of debt, we free ourselves to focus on what truly matters: loving and supporting one another.

In this chapter, we'll explore the importance of paying bills on time, strategies to get out of debt, and how automating your finances can bring peace, freedom, and better relationships.

The Importance of Paying Bills on Time

Paying bills on time is more than just a financial responsibility—it's a commitment to integrity and stewardship. Here's why it matters:

Avoiding Financial Penalties:

- Late payments often come with fees or penalties, which can quickly add up. These costs reduce the money you have for other priorities and can make it harder to break free from financial stress.

Protecting Your Credit Score:

- Consistently paying bills on time is one of the biggest factors in maintaining a good credit score. A strong credit score opens doors to better financial opportunities, like lower interest rates and access to credit when needed.

Maintaining Good Relationships:

- Whether it's your landlord, utility provider, or a friend you borrowed from, paying what you owe on time shows respect and reliability. It helps maintain trust and avoids the tension that comes with overdue payments.

Reducing Stress:

- Late bills and mounting debt can weigh heavily on your mind, leading to sleepless nights and strained relationships. Paying bills on time gives you peace of mind and allows you to focus on more meaningful aspects of life.

Getting Out of Debt: Breaking the Chains

Debt can feel like a heavy burden, but it's possible to break free with a plan and determination. Here are steps to help you get out of debt:

Face the Numbers:

- Start by listing all your debts, including balances, interest rates, and minimum payments. Knowing where you stand is the first step to creating a plan.

Prioritize Your Debts:

- Use strategies like the **debt snowball** (paying off the smallest debts first for quick wins) or the **debt avalanche** (paying off the highest-interest debts first to save money over time). Choose the method that feels most motivating to you.

Cut Unnecessary Expenses:

- Look for areas in your budget where you can reduce spending. Redirect those savings toward paying down debt faster.

Earn Extra Income:

- Consider side gigs, selling unused items, or taking on overtime at work to generate additional income that you can put toward debt repayment.

Celebrate Milestones:

- As you pay off each debt, celebrate your progress. Acknowledge the hard work you've done to move closer to financial freedom.

The Power of Automating Your Bills

One of the simplest ways to stay on top of your finances is to automate your bill payments. Here's how automation can transform your financial life:

Eliminates the Risk of Forgetting:

- When you automate your payments, you never have to worry about missing a due date. Your bills are paid on time, every time.

Reduces Stress and Saves Time:

- Automation takes the mental load off your shoulders. You no longer need to track multiple due dates or set reminders—it's all handled for you.

Improves Financial Discipline:

- Automated payments ensure that your obligations are met first before you're tempted to spend on non-essentials. This keeps your priorities in check.

Helps You Focus on What Matters:

- With your bills taken care of, you're free to focus on the bigger picture—like spending time with loved ones, pursuing your goals, and deepening your relationships.

The Connection Between Financial Health and Relationships

Romans 13:8 reminds us that our primary obligation is to love one another. When we're overwhelmed by unpaid bills and debt, it's hard to give our best to the people around us. Financial stress can lead to arguments, distraction, and feelings of guilt or inadequacy. On the other hand, when we're financially stable, we can show up fully for the people we care about.

Paying bills on time and getting out of debt also allows us to be more generous. With fewer financial burdens, we have the freedom to give—whether that's helping a friend in need, supporting a cause we're passionate about, or simply creating joyful experiences for our family.

Conclusion: Freedom to Focus on Love

Automating your bill payments and working toward debt freedom is about more than just managing money—it's about creating space in your life to focus on what truly matters. When you no longer owe anyone anything, you're free to fulfill the higher purpose of loving and serving others, as Paul encourages us in Romans 13:8.

Imagine a life where you wake up each day knowing your bills are paid, your debts are decreasing, and your finances are under control. That's a life where you can fully embrace your relationships, pursue your passions, and contribute to the world around you. It's a life of peace, purpose, and abundance—and it starts with one simple step: paying your bills on time.

Take action today. Automate your payments, create a plan to tackle your debt, and let go of the stress that's been holding you back. With each step, you'll move closer to financial freedom and a life focused on what matters most.

CHAPTER 5: DOLLAR COST AVERAGING (AUTOMATE INVESTMENTS)

"Cast your bread upon the waters, for you will find it after many days" (Ecclesiastes 11:1). Investing wisely and diversely yields returns over time.

Step-by-Step:

1. *Choose an Investment Platform: Select a brokerage or robo-advisor that offers automated investing.*
2. *Set Up Automatic Contributions: Arrange for regular transfers to your investment accounts.*
3. *Diversify: Ensure your investments are diversified to spread risk.*

Casting Your Bread Upon The Waters: The Power Of Automating Your Investments

Investing For The Future

Ecclesiastes 11:1 says, "Cast your bread upon the waters, for you will find it after many days." This verse, often interpreted as a call to generosity and wise planning, also contains timeless wisdom about investing. It speaks to the principle of planting seeds today to reap benefits in the future, a concept at the heart of building wealth through investments.

Investing can feel overwhelming, especially if you're new to it. But with the right tools and strategies, you can automate your investments and make consistent progress toward your financial goals. Whether you have a pension, 401(k), or other retirement plans, diversifying your investments is crucial for long-term stability and growth.

In this chapter, we'll walk through the importance of automating your investments, how to get started, and why even small, sustainable contributions can have a significant impact over time.

Why Automating Your Investments Matters

Consistency is Key:

- Regularly investing, no matter how small the amount, allows you to benefit from the power of **compound growth**. By automating your contributions, you ensure that you're consistently building wealth over time without relying on willpower.

Reduces Emotional Decisions:

- Investing can be intimidating, especially during market volatility. Automation removes the temptation to make emotional decisions, like pulling out of the market when prices drop or trying to time your investments.

Maximizes Time in the Market:

- A common saying in investing is, *"Time in the market beats timing the market."* Starting early and contributing consistently allows your investments to grow exponentially, thanks to compounding returns.

Diversifies Your Income Sources:

- Even if you have a pension, Social Security, or other retirement income, having a diversified investment portfolio ensures you're not overly reliant on one source. This reduces risk and provides additional financial security.

Getting Started: Automating Your Investments

If you're new to investing, follow these steps to get started:

1. **Open a Brokerage Account**
   a. **Choose a Platform:** Select a brokerage that fits your needs. Look for features like low fees, an intuitive interface, and automation tools. Examples include Fidelity, Vanguard, Schwab, or online platforms like Robinhood or M1 Finance.
   b. **Provide Documentation:** You'll need basic personal information, a Social Security number, and a funding source (like a checking

account) to open an account.

2. **Choose an Investment Vehicle**
    a. **Index Funds and ETFs:** Low-cost index funds or exchange-traded funds (ETFs) are great options for beginners. They provide instant diversification by investing in a broad market index, like the S&P 500.
    b. **Target-Date Funds:** If you're investing for retirement, consider a target-date fund that automatically adjusts its asset allocation as you approach your retirement date.
    c. **Individual Stocks:** For those comfortable with more risk and research, investing in individual stocks can provide higher growth potential.
    d. **Robo-Advisors:** Platforms like Betterment or Wealthfront can create and manage a diversified portfolio for you based on your goals and risk tolerance.
3. **Set Up Automated Contributions**
    a. **Determine a Sustainable Amount:** Review your budget and decide how much you can comfortably contribute to your investments each month. Even starting with $50 or $100 per month can make a difference over time.
    b. **Link Your Bank Account:** Set up automatic transfers from your checking or savings account to your brokerage account. Schedule the transfers for a consistent day each month, such as after payday.
    c. **Automate the Investments:** Most brokerages allow you to automate the process of investing in specific funds or stocks. This ensures your money is working for you immediately, rather

than sitting idle in cash.

4. **Diversify Your Investments**
   a. **Spread Your Risk:** Invest in a mix of asset classes (stocks, bonds, and real estate) across different industries and geographic regions.
   b. **Consider Retirement Accounts:** Max out contributions to tax-advantaged accounts like IRAs or 401(k)s before focusing on taxable brokerage accounts.

5. **Monitor and Adjust Periodically**
   a. **Check Your Progress:** While automation makes investing easy, review your accounts periodically to ensure your portfolio aligns with your goals and risk tolerance.
   b. **Rebalance as Needed:** Over time, your asset allocation may drift due to market performance. Rebalancing ensures your portfolio stays aligned with your original plan.

Sustainable Contributions: The Key to Success

Many people hesitate to invest because they feel like they don't have "enough" money. But the truth is, small, consistent contributions add up over time. Here's how to determine a sustainable amount to invest:

1. **Start Small:**
   a. Begin with what you can afford, even if it's just $20 a month. The important thing is to start.
2. **Increase Over Time:**
   a. As your income grows or you pay off debts, increase your contributions. Even a small increase—like an extra $10 or $20 a month —can significantly impact your long-term growth.

3. **Make it a Priority:**
    a. Treat investing like any other bill. By automating your contributions, you're prioritizing your future self just as you prioritize paying your rent or utilities.

The Ripple Effect of Automated Investments

Automating your investments doesn't just benefit your finances—it can optimize your entire life:

1. **Peace of Mind:**
    a. Knowing you're consistently building wealth reduces financial stress and allows you to focus on other areas of life, like relationships, personal growth, and hobbies.
2. **More Time and Energy:**
    a. Automation eliminates the need to manually transfer funds or decide when and where to invest. This frees up mental energy for more meaningful activities.
3. **A Sense of Accomplishment:**
    a. Watching your investments grow over time gives you a sense of progress and motivation to continue working toward your financial goals.
4. **Generational Impact:**
    a. Automated investing helps you build a legacy. Whether it's passing on wealth to your children or supporting causes you care about, the choices you make today can benefit generations to come.

Practical Exercise: Start Automating Your Investments TODAY!

1. **Set Your Goal:**
    a. Write down one long-term financial goal, such as saving for retirement, buying a home, or building a college fund.
2. **Calculate Your Contribution:**

   a. Determine how much you can comfortably invest each month. Start small if necessary and increase over time.
3. **Choose Your Platform:**
   a. Research and select a brokerage or robo-advisor that fits your needs.
4. **Automate the Process:**
   a. Set up automated transfers and investments through your chosen platform.
5. **Review Annually:**
   a. Schedule an annual check-in to assess your progress and adjust your contributions or portfolio as needed.

Conclusion: Casting Your Bread Upon the Waters

The wisdom of Ecclesiastes 11:1 reminds us that investing is an act of faith and preparation. When you automate your investments, you're planting seeds that will grow over time, ensuring that you're building a secure and abundant future.

Remember, it's not about how much you start with—it's about starting. By taking small, consistent steps and automating the process, you'll create a financial foundation that allows you to live with confidence, freedom, and peace of mind. So cast your bread upon the waters, and trust that your efforts will yield returns in due time.

Automating your investments is a simple yet transformative step that aligns your financial actions with your long-term goals. It ensures that you're consistently building wealth, reducing stress, and freeing up your time to focus on what truly matters.

Remember, the act of investing isn't just about accumulating money—it's about creating a foundation for the life you want to live. It's about being a good steward of the resources you've been given and using them to secure your future.

Take that first step today. Open your brokerage account, choose your investments, and automate your contributions. Cast your bread upon the waters, and watch as your efforts come back to you many times over, enriching not just your financial life but every aspect of your journey.

CHAPTER 6: CHECK AND ADJUST

"The heart of the discerning acquires knowledge, for the ears of the wise seek it out" (Proverbs 18:15). Continual learning and adjustment are key to effective financial stewardship.

Step-by-Step:

1. *Review Your Automated Systems: Regularly check that your automatic transfers and payments are working as intended.*
2. *Adjust as Needed: Modify amounts or add new goals as your financial situation changes.*
3. *Stay Informed: Keep up with financial news and trends to make informed decisions.*

Wisdom And Wealth: The Art Of Continual Learning And Adjustment

Financial Stewardship Requires Intention

Proverbs 18:15 says, "The heart of the discerning acquires knowledge, for the ears of the wise seek it out." This verse reminds us that wisdom is not static—it's something we actively pursue. In the same way, managing your financial life is not a one-time task. It's a process of continual learning, intentional adjustments, and growth.

While automation is a powerful tool to simplify your finances, it's not an excuse to put your financial life on autopilot. Think of automation as a system you design with intention. Over time, the system becomes more efficient, but you still need to check in periodically to ensure it's working as intended.

This chapter explores why continual learning and adjustment are essential to financial stewardship and offers practical guidance to help you stay intentional, adapt to life's changes, and maintain control over your financial future.

Automating with Intention

When you automate your finances, you create a framework that helps you stay on track with minimal effort. But even the best systems need oversight. Here's why intentionality is so important:

Avoiding "Set and Forget" Pitfalls:

- Automation without intention can lead to overlooked opportunities or costly mistakes. For example, you might continue paying for subscriptions you no longer use or neglect to adjust your savings rate as your income grows.

Fine-Tuning for Life Changes:

- Life is full of changes—new jobs, family milestones, market shifts, and unexpected expenses. Your financial system should evolve with your circumstances.

Building Confidence and Knowledge:

- Regularly reviewing and adjusting your finances helps you understand your money better. Over time, this builds confidence and reduces stress, allowing you to make informed decisions even when life throws curveballs.

The Cycle of Learning and Adjusting

1. **Start with a Plan:**
    a. In the early stages of building your financial system, be hands-on. Understand your budget, set financial goals, and choose investments that align with those goals.
2. **Automate and Observe:**
    a. Once your system is in place, let automation handle the day-to-day tasks like bill payments, savings contributions, and investments. Use this time to observe how the system works and identify areas for improvement.
3. **Review Regularly:**
    a. Schedule periodic check-ins—monthly, quarterly, or annually—to review your accounts, spending, and progress toward your goals. Ask yourself:
    b. Are you meeting your savings and investment targets?
    c. Do your spending habits align with your values and goals?
    d. Are there any unnecessary expenses you can eliminate?
4. **Adjust as Needed:**
    a. Make adjustments based on your findings. This could mean increasing your retirement

contributions after a raise, reallocating your investments to match your risk tolerance, or creating a new savings goal for a major life event.

5. **Educate Yourself:**
    a. Stay informed about personal finance by reading books, listening to podcasts, or taking online courses. The more you learn, the better equipped you'll be to make adjustments and optimize your financial life.

The Long-Term Benefits of Financial Stewardship

Over time, the process of learning and adjusting becomes second nature. Here are the long-term benefits of this approach:

Resilience During Life's Changes:

- Whether it's a job loss, a market downturn, or an unexpected expense, a well-maintained financial system gives you the flexibility and resources to adapt without panic.

Maximized Opportunities:

- Regularly reviewing your finances allows you to spot opportunities, like taking advantage of employer benefits, refinancing a loan for better terms, or investing in high-growth opportunities.

Freedom to Focus on What Matters:

- When your financial system runs smoothly, you can spend less time worrying about money and more time focusing on your relationships, passions, and personal growth.

Confidence in Your Financial Future:

- As you gain knowledge and experience, you'll feel more confident in your ability to handle financial decisions, no matter what challenges arise.

Practical Steps for Continual Learning and Adjustment

Schedule Financial Check-Ins:

- Set aside time every quarter or year to review your financial system. Use this time to evaluate your progress, adjust your goals, and refine your plan.

Track Your Progress:

- Use financial tools or apps to track your net worth, spending, and investment performance. Seeing your progress can be incredibly motivating.

Stay Informed:

- Make it a habit to read books, follow financial blogs, or attend workshops on personal finance. Staying informed keeps you ahead of the curve.

Work with a Financial Coach:

- A financial coach can provide guidance, help you set realistic goals, and hold you accountable. They can also offer fresh perspectives and strategies to optimize your system.

Celebrate Milestones:

- Recognize your achievements along the way, whether it's paying off a debt, reaching a savings goal, or making your first investment. Celebrating keeps you motivated and reinforces positive habits.

A Story of Adjustment and Growth

When Sarah first automated her finances, she felt a sense of relief. Her bills were paid on time, her savings were growing, and her investments were on autopilot. But a year later, she realized she hadn't checked her accounts in months. When she finally did, she noticed some issues: she was still paying for a gym membership she no longer used, her savings rate hadn't increased despite a recent raise, and her investment portfolio was too conservative for her long-term goals.

Instead of feeling discouraged, Sarah saw this as an opportunity to fine-tune her system. She canceled unnecessary subscriptions, increased her savings contributions, and adjusted her investment allocations to match her growing confidence and knowledge. Over time, these small adjustments had a big impact. Sarah's finances not only improved, but she also felt more in control and less stressed.

Conclusion: Intentional Stewardship Brings Peace

Proverbs 18:15 teaches us that wise stewardship requires continual learning and growth. Your financial journey is not a "set it and forget it" process—it's an ongoing relationship with your money that evolves as you do.

By automating your finances with intention, reviewing them regularly, and staying committed to learning, you're not just managing money—you're building a life of stability, confidence, and freedom. Over time, these habits will become second nature, and the adjustments you make will feel less like a burden and more like an opportunity to fine-tune your financial future.

Remember, you don't have to do this alone. Books like this, financial tools, and experienced coaches are here to guide you. With intention and effort, you'll develop the wisdom and resilience to navigate life's financial curveballs and enjoy the peace that comes from being a good steward of your resources.

CHAPTER 7: REFLECTING AND GIVING THANKS

"And whatever you do, whether in word or deed, do it all in the name of the Lord Jesus, giving thanks to God the Father through him" (Colossians 3:17). Recognizing and being grateful for your progress is important.

Step-by-Step:

1. *Reflect on Your Progress: Take time to see how far you've come in automating your finances.*
2. *Give Thanks: Appreciate the discipline and tools that have helped you along the way.*
3. *Share Your Success: Consider sharing your knowledge and helping others automate their financial lives.*

Reflecting, Giving Thanks, And Planting With Faith

A Heart Of Gratitude

As you work through building your financial life and creating systems that automate, grow, and protect your resources, it's important to take a step back and reflect. Colossians 3:17 reminds us: "And whatever you do, whether in word or deed, do it all in the name of the Lord Jesus, giving thanks to God the Father through him." This verse calls us to live with intention and gratitude, acknowledging that all our efforts, achievements, and blessings ultimately flow from God.

Our financial systems may seem technical and practical, but they should also reflect our values, faith, and gratitude. This chapter explores the importance of reflecting on your journey, giving thanks for your progress, and planting seeds of faith that will lead to a fruitful harvest.

Reflection: Celebrate the Journey

It's easy to focus on what still needs to be done—the goals you haven't reached or the setbacks you've faced. But reflection is about looking at how far you've come, not just how far you have left to go.

Why Reflection Matters:

Recognize Your Growth:

- Every small step forward is progress. By reflecting on your journey, you can see how your efforts—like automating savings or reducing debt—are bearing fruit over time.

Build Confidence:

- When you acknowledge your achievements, you build confidence in your ability to handle future challenges. Reflection reminds you that you're capable of making wise financial decisions.

Stay Motivated:

- Celebrating milestones, even small ones, keeps you motivated to continue the work. Reflection is a way of fueling your spirit and staying focused on the bigger picture.

Practical Reflection Exercise:

Monthly Reflection Questions:

- What financial wins did I experience this month?
- How have my habits changed since I started this journey?
- What lessons did I learn from any challenges I faced?

Celebrate Wins:

- Treat yourself to something simple—a favorite meal, a walk in nature, or time with loved ones—as a way of celebrating your progress.

Giving Thanks: Recognizing the Source of Your Blessings

While your hard work and discipline play a significant role in your financial success, it's important to remember that every opportunity, every resource, and every bit of wisdom comes from God. Gratitude is a way of acknowledging that truth and keeping your heart grounded.

Why Gratitude is Essential:

Keeps You Humble:

- Gratitude reminds us that we don't achieve success on our own. It's a partnership between our efforts and God's provision.

Shifts Your Focus:

- When you focus on what you're grateful for, you're less likely to dwell on what you lack. Gratitude helps you see abundance, not scarcity.

Strengthens Your Faith:

- Expressing thanks reinforces your trust in God's plan and His ability to provide for your needs.

Ways to Practice Gratitude:

1. **Daily Prayer:**
   a. Begin or end your day by thanking God for specific blessings—your job, your health, your family, or the wisdom to make better financial choices.
2. **Gratitude Journal:**
   a. Write down three things you're thankful for each day. Over time, this habit helps you cultivate a more grateful perspective.
3. **Give Back:**
   a. Use your blessings to bless others. Whether it's through tithing, volunteering, or supporting a cause you care about, giving is a tangible way to express gratitude.

Planting with Faith: Trusting the Process

Reflecting and giving thanks are not just about looking back—they're also about planting seeds for the future. When farmers plant their crops, they don't control the weather or the soil conditions. They plant in faith, trusting that their labor will yield a harvest. In the same way, managing your finances requires faith in the principles you're following and trust in God's provision.

The Principles of Planting with Faith:

Follow Sound Practices:

- Just as farmers prepare the soil and plant at the right time, you're following proven financial principles—automating savings, investing, paying off debt, and living within your means.

Trust the Process:

- Results don't happen overnight. Trust that your consistent efforts will bear fruit over time, even when you can't see immediate results.

Adapt to Change:

- Life's "weather" isn't always predictable—unexpected expenses, market shifts, or personal challenges can arise. But with faith and good stewardship, you can adjust and continue to plant seeds of growth.

Scripture and Faith in Action:

Ecclesiastes 11:6: *"Sow your seed in the morning, and at evening let your hands not be idle, for you do not know which will succeed, whether this or that, or whether both will do equally well."*

- This verse reminds us that success comes from consistent effort and trust, even when outcomes aren't guaranteed.

A Balanced System: Work, Faith, and Gratitude

Your financial system should be more than just a technical framework—it should reflect your faith and values. Here's how to create a balanced system that incorporates work, faith, and gratitude:

1. **Start with Intention:**
    a. Align your financial goals with your values and purpose. Whether it's providing for your family, giving to your community, or achieving financial independence, keep your "why" at the center.
2. **Automate with Care:**
    a. Automation simplifies your life, but don't let it lead to complacency. Regularly review your system to ensure it reflects your current goals and priorities.
3. **Reflect and Adjust:**
    a. Make reflection a regular practice. Use it as a time to celebrate progress, learn from challenges, and fine-tune your system.
4. **Give Thanks Regularly:**
    a. Incorporate gratitude into your daily life, both through prayer and action. Recognize the blessings you've received and use them to bless others.
5. **Have Faith in the Process:**
    a. Trust that your consistent efforts, guided by sound principles, will lead to a harvest in due time. Remember, it's not just about the money—it's about building a life of purpose, generosity, and peace.

Conclusion: Reflect, Give Thanks, and Keep Planting

The journey to financial freedom and stewardship is not just about building wealth—it's about building character, faith, and gratitude along the way. Colossians 3:17 reminds us to do everything with gratitude and intention, giving glory to God for every blessing and achievement.

As you reflect on your journey, give yourself credit for the hard work you've done. Acknowledge the challenges you've overcome and celebrate the progress you've made. But above all, give God the glory for guiding you, providing for you, and sustaining you.

Continue planting seeds of faith through sound financial principles, and trust that the harvest will come. Life may not always go as planned, but with reflection, gratitude, and faith, you'll have the tools to navigate whatever comes your way. As your financial system becomes a source of stability and peace, you'll find even greater freedom to focus on what truly matters—loving God, loving others, and living a life of purpose.

REVIEW: BUILDING A FINANCIAL LIFE OF STEWARDSHIP AND FAITH

Building A Financial Life Of Stewardship And Faith

Congratulations! By following this seven-day plan, you've taken intentional steps to automate your financial life, set meaningful goals, and embrace principles of stewardship that honor both your values and your faith. These steps may seem small at first, but they lay the foundation for a secure, prosperous, and purpose-driven financial future.

The journey you've embarked on isn't just about money—it's about creating a system that reflects diligence, planning, and gratitude. It's about being a faithful steward of the resources entrusted to you and ensuring that your financial life aligns with the life you want to build.

Proverbs 3:9-10 beautifully ties it all together: "Honor the Lord with your wealth, with the first fruits of all your crops; then your barns will be filled to overflowing, and your vats will brim over with new wine." This scripture reminds us that when we manage our finances with intention, integrity, and gratitude, we honor God and position ourselves to experience His blessings.

Summarized Step-by-Step Reference:
Here's a quick recap of the steps you've learned, making it easy to reference and apply them to your daily life:

1. **Financial Goals (Day 1):**
    a. Write down your short-term, medium-term, and long-term goals. Prioritize them based on what matters most to you.
    b. Reflect on Luke 14:28, planning your financial "tower" with a clear purpose.
2. **Create a Budget (Day 2):**
    a. Replace the term "budget" with a Life Plan to focus on making intentional choices that align with your values.
    b. Track your expenses, categorize them, and ensure your spending reflects your priorities.
3. **Automate Savings (Day 3):**
    a. Open a dedicated savings account and set up automatic transfers to build your emergency fund and save for future goals.
    b. Remember Proverbs 21:20: The wise store up resources for the future.
4. **Automate Bill Payments (Day 4):**
    a. Set up automated payments for recurring bills to avoid late fees and stress, ensuring your financial obligations are met.
    b. Reflect on Romans 13:8, freeing yourself to focus on loving others by living debt-free.
5. **Automate Investments (Day 5):**
    a. Open a brokerage account, choose diversified investments like index funds or ETFs, and automate regular contributions.
    b. Follow Ecclesiastes 11:1: Cast your bread upon the waters, trusting in the harvest that comes

with consistency.

6. **Review and Adjust Regularly (Day 6):**
   a. Schedule regular financial check-ins to ensure your system is working and aligns with your changing goals and circumstances.
   b. Proverbs 18:15 encourages us to continually seek knowledge and discernment.
7. **Reflect, Give Thanks, and Trust (Day 7):**
   a. Make gratitude and reflection a regular part of your financial journey. Acknowledge your progress, give thanks to God, and trust in His provision.
   b. Colossians 3:17 reminds us to do everything with gratitude, honoring God through our work.

A Final Encouragement

This seven-day journey is just the beginning. I should also add, that whether you complete these steps over a literal 7 days, 7 months, or even 7 years, your progress is your progress. We talked about it earlier, the great thing about principles is that they work, whenever we decide to utilize them. The important thing is to start; as you continue to implement these steps and adjust your system, you'll find that managing your finances becomes less stressful and more empowering. Remember that life will bring changes and challenges, but with a foundation built on diligence, planning, and gratitude, you'll be well-equipped to navigate them.

Your financial life is a reflection of your values, faith, and choices. By automating your finances and practicing good stewardship, you're not just building wealth—you're building a legacy of wisdom, generosity, and purpose.

So as you go forward, let the principles you've learned guide you. Honor the Lord with your wealth, stay diligent in your efforts, and trust that the seeds you plant today will yield a harvest of peace, security, and fulfillment in the future.

Your journey to financial freedom and stewardship begins today. Keep planting, keep reflecting, and keep trusting.

The best is yet to come.

ABOUT THE AUTHOR

Richard Frierson is a dedicated financial coach, educator, and advocate for breaking the cycles of financial struggle and creating generational wealth. With a background in financial coaching and a deep understanding of the emotional and behavioral aspects of money, he has dedicated their career to helping individuals and families shift their mindsets, take control of their finances, and build a future rooted in financial stability and abundance.

Growing up, Richard witnessed firsthand how financial stress can impact individuals, relationships, and communities. Determined to break the cycle, they embarked on their journey toward financial literacy—learning, experimenting, and developing strategies that not only transformed their finances but also allowed them to guide others toward lasting financial success. From navigating debt, mastering budgeting (or what they call a Life Plan), and building wealth through investing, Richard has used real-world experience and tested principles to help others reclaim their financial power.

With years of experience coaching individuals from all walks of life—whether it's those struggling to make ends meet, professionals looking to optimize their wealth, or families seeking to change their financial legacy—he believes that financial freedom is not just about numbers. It's about mindset, discipline, and applying timeless principles of stewardship and wealth-building.

This book is an extension of that mission. Through faith-based wisdom, practical strategies, and actionable steps, Richard equips readers with the tools they need to automate their finances, eliminate debt, invest wisely, and, most importantly, live with intention and purpose.

When he's not coaching or writing, Richard enjoys traveling with his family, exploring financial literacy through different cultural perspectives, and empowering others to live life on their terms. The ultimate goal? To see more people—especially those who have felt financially stuck—step into a life of freedom, wealth, and impact.

Connect with Richard Frierson @esinnovationinc@gmail.com for more financial insights, resources, and coaching opportunities at https://es-innovation-inc.square.site.

Made in the USA
Monee, IL
04 November 2026

67387147R00036